Are English Jews Responsible for 9/11?

Are English Jews Responsible for 9/11?

An Examination of the History, Problems, and Causes

The Hermit Kingdom Press
Cheltenham   Seoul   Bangalore   Cebu

Are English Jews Responsible for 9/11?
An Examination of the History, Problems, and Causes

Copyright © 2004 by Devdas Pradesh

ISBN 1-59689-006-1 (hardcover)
ISBN 1-59689-007-X (paperback)

(USA) Library of Congress Control Number: 2004116183

Write-To Address:

The Hermit Kingdom Press
3741 Walnut Street, Suite 407
Philadelphia, PA 19104
United States of America

Info@TheHermitKingdomPress.com

★ ★ ★ ★

Hermit Kingdom
12 South Bridge, Suite 370
Edinburgh, EH1 1DD
Scotland

http://www.TheHermitKingdomPress.com

Dedicated to the American People

Content

"No man can sit down and withhold his hands from the warfare against wrong and get peace from his acquiescence."

28th US President Woodrow Wilson
(1856-1924)

Introduction

September 11, 2001, will forever be ingrained in the American psyche as a critical point in American history. The attacks on Washington, DC, and New York City were not devastating only in terms of numbers. As great as a few thousand deaths are, America has lost many more lives in other wars, including wars fought on American soil, like the American Revolutionary War and the Civil War.

However, what made September 11th so devastating was the fact that America was taken by a surprise attack. There was a sense that there was unfair play involved. No one officially declared war. Some people sneaked into American private property and destroyed what Americans treasured the most – the American sense of security and peace.

It can be explained in light of Pearl Harbor. Like September 11th, there were not many deaths in comparison to other incidents involving warfare. However, what angered the American people was the lack of fair play. The sneak attack seemed like an underhanded way to screw someone over with no regard for decency. It's like a friend stealing your girlfriend while pretending to support you in your love interest. It's like your trusted friend depreciating the value of your net worth through underhanded means – such as passing your private information to those who can and will use it against you

– when this friend should be dedicated to preserving your net worth (or even increasing it).

Pearl Harbor represented a supposed friend acting worse than an enemy. It wasn't the number of people who were killed that angered Americans. It was the fundamental sense of deprivation of fair play that incensed Americans. Americans believed that they were crying out for justice at the unfairness of it all, more than for revenge (although revenge was an important part of it). The war took on a moral discourse that justified retribution few thousand times greater than the perpetrated wrong.

It was the very sense that Americans had been ill-treated and the "game" manipulated unfairly that made Americans sleep soundly at night knowing that Atom Bombs killed hundreds of thousands of innocent civilians at a blink of an eye. The sense of justice and fair play justified genocide in American popular psyche and in American government policy.

It is safe to assume that Americans do not buy into an-eye-for-an-eye principle when they feel that fair play has been tainted. Americans rather subscribe to the-whole-body-for-an-eye policy of retribution. The Atom Bombs killed many more than the number of unexpecting Americans killed in Pearl Harbor. Most Americans will not be embarrassed to say that this was an equitable settlement. It is the divestiture of fair play that changed the equation in terms of numbers.

One might equal one in a void, in the absence of a sneak-attack. But in the presence of unfair play, one does not equal one. In the presence of cold-blooded betrayal, Americans who emerged from Pearl Harbor were willing to make one equal infinity.

September 11, 2001, is, in many ways, similar. Americans fundamentally feel that there was unfair play involved. There was no public (or private) declaration of war on American soil. The fact that anyone can highjack a plane and destroy innocent lives seemed unfathomable to the American sense of fair play. 9/11 represented a sneak-attack that seemed to violate all that is decent in the world. And 9/11 captured the collective anger of the American people.

In light of the American perception that unfair play was involved and justice had to be done, it is not surprising that President George W. Bush initially named the retribution campaign, "Operation Infinite Justice." There was a sense in Washington, DC, and generally among the American populace that nothing short of infinite justice would do. One did not equal one. In the presence of the violation of all that is decent, one equalled infinity.

Thus, it is not surprising that when President George W. Bush decided immediately to go to war, the Senate gave him its unanimous support. The US Senate believed President Bush to be the decisive Commander-in-Chief, and praises flowed from distinguished Republican Senators as well as well-respected Democratic Senators. A retribution campaign had to be done. It would have been un-American not to retaliate against the evil that threatened fairness and justice. George W. Bush was right to declare war and seek "infinite justice."

Some have even said that even if some Senators did not personally believe in a retaliatory war, if they did not support Bush, their opposition will result in the end of their political career. Given the fact Bush enjoyed general support of the populace (some saying up to 90% of the popular support for war), the analysis is probably right on the mark. Americans wanted blood, pure and simple. Unfair play was done. The bastards sneaked into American property and attacked in the most unrespectable manner possible, and they had to pay for it.

The majority of the Americans were resolved that it was a moral issue to seek blood. The discourse in the American public scene was that the retaliatory war was an ethical act that was crucial for restoring the value of decency and respectability to the nation. The perpetrators had to be punished, and they had to be punished visibly and violently.

Indeed, President Bush probably could have dropped a few nuclear bombs on Afghanistan, and he would have enjoyed predominant support of the American people right after September 11, 2001. Americans have proven time and time again through actual practice that they do not have a fundamental problem with genocidal tactics in warfare. For many Americans, justice is the highest value, and unfair play must be punished.

Anything less would be appeasement. And the fundamental philosophy of Americans is that it is better to commit genocides than appease the violators involved in unfair play. The sentiment of righteous retribution is so strong in America that it can be seen as an integral part of the American psyche. America's very character as America is wrapped up in the understanding the righteous retribution must be done in the event of unfair play.

Thus, it is not surprising that a person who barely won the presidency came to enjoy nearly 90% approval rating. Americans fundamentally believe in retributive justice, even using genocidal violence, and President George W. Bush was willing to act as the representative leader of the American people. Post-9/11,

Americans saw in George W. Bush "the Everyman," or "the Every-American." President Bush, his harsh, vindictive rhetoric, and decisive revenge through war represented the sentiment and the wish of most Americans.

Even Chelsea Clinton spoke up at Oxford University in support of the American war initiated by President George W. Bush and was reported to have been harassed by English students at Oxford for her position. Chelsea Clinton's interview with American media highlighted for the American youth the fundamental difference between English students and Americans students when it comes to retributive wars for the sake of "justice" in lieu of unfair play.

Some argue that if September 11, 2001, happened in London and Edinburgh, the response of the British to protect their value and security would have mirrored the American response. The fact that 9/11 did not happen in London and Edinburgh makes it hard to speak conclusively about the British response. For America, the response among the college students mirrored general popular sentiment and the leadership of President George W. Bush.

Besides a type of homogeneity in support of a revenge war, 9/11 produced in America another phenomena. Since the incident, there has been numerous writing from all segments of society regarding (and reacting to) the incident. The preponderance of writing on the subject is so numerous as to redefine the American character specifically around the incident. The most predictable result of the whole process is questioning of certain policies and ideas that made America susceptible to September 11th attacks.

In other words, while America sought to seek revenge for 9/11, Americans vented their anger constructively by looking for causes. Some have negatively assessed the trend as "the blame game" or "conspiracy theories." However, as many Americans are fundamentally keen to make things right and to prevent such occurrences in the future, the search for causes has gained tremendous popular support.

There has been general critical examination of American security institutions, such as the CIA and the FBI. There has even been grossly critical examination of what might have gone wrong within these institutions to allow for such a tragic incident. New security agencies were created to fill in the gaps that allowed for the tragedy to occur. There is a general trend to correct the elements that devalued America's worth as a secure nation in the eyes of the international community.

In the midst of all the critical thinking on the causes, many Americans, both intellectuals and ordinary folks, have turned their attention to the Middle East. After all, the terrorists came from the Middle East, so the reasons for terror attacks can be found there. Isn't this the logical way to look for causes?

General popular discourse, both on the right and the left, in America right now is that Americans must assume that the American policy in the Middle East in the past 50 years or so was grossly in error. Such discourse can be heard everywhere among Americans in debate chambers as well as in bar settings. The fact that the terrorists seem to say, "Death to Israel! Death to America!" in the same breath has encouraged ordinary Americans as well as policy makers to think about Israel as an important cause for making America into a target. After all, the terrorists are making the link, so there must be a direct link in their minds for terrorist attacks they want to carry out in America.

The American government has been quite quick to respond. There have been investigations of even high ranking Pentagon officials of spying for Israel. It can be seen as a way America is sending message to both outsiders and insiders. Accusing high ranking Pentagon officials of spying for Israel and potentially putting them in jail for a life-term sentence sends the message to the outsiders that America does not support Israel.

Sending the message that America does not support Israel will discourage terrorism on account of Israel. If America can convince the terrorists that America does not support Israel, then the terrorists will no longer say, "Death to Israel! Death to America!" in the same breath. They will eventually only say, "Death to Israel!" For the sake of defending America, such a trend would suit the American people just fine since they want peace and security on American soil.

Furthermore, the US government investigation of high ranking Pentagon officials on the charge of spying for Israel sends a message to insiders. The American government wants to emphasize to pro-Israeli elements in American military, security forces, and the government that an aggressive pro-Israel stance could bring down criminal investigation. It is a way to clamp down on the security threat that may exist within the US government structure and affiliated institutions.

Many understand the measure to be directed particularly Jews as American Jews have a long history of supporting the State of Israel and lobbying for Israel. The American charge of spying for Israel will discourage American Jews, particularly in America, of open and aggressive support of the Jewish nation in the Middle East that the terrorists cite as the reason for attacks on

America. Put in a blunt way, accusing a high ranking Pentagon official of spying for Israel is a way to reduce "the threat from within" (whether intentional or unintentional on the part of those who are aggressively pro-Israel).

It is true that Israel is probably at the heart of the problem of global terrorism as Americans experienced on September 11, 2001. The suspicion that there are American high ranking officials who may spy for Israel highlights the fact that not only is the State of Israel itself a potential threat to the degeneration in the affair of the War on Terrorism, but that a real threat exists within America itself for the exacerbation of the situation. Potential elements for increasing terror threat are perceived to be already present in America.

There is increasingly discussion and writing on the subject. However, a similar type of discussion and discourse does not exist in England. England has not accused any high ranking English official of spying for Israel, although there is a greater likelihood of spying for Israel in England than in the USA, given the history.

This book is an effort to correct the gap in critical thinking about September 11, 2001. No critical thinking about the causes of the 9/11 attacks is complete without at least raising the question of English Jewish involvement in the causes, whether inadvertently or intentionally.

This book raises the question and attempts to answer them. As there are not many books on this subject, this book may be seen as an initial investigation on the question. However, I hope that this book will provide complete enough discussion to allow the readers to fill in the gaps of the questions regarding the causes to the September 11th attacks.

More importantly, I hope that my book will serve the constructive purpose of adding to making America (and the United Kingdom) more secure and safe for their citizens. If this book can help save thousands (of millions?) of American and British lives, by helping policy makers to fill in some of their gaps in information that are relevant to the War on Terrorism, then I would consider my book a complete success.

So, I would like now to state the question explicitly. Are English Jews responsible for September 11th? If so, in what way? And to what extent?

THE HOLOCAUST

Some may question the very foundation of the right to question the possibility that English Jews are somehow responsible for September 11th attacks. Are Jews not victims after all? We are, after all, talking about people who experienced the loss of 6 million lives in the Holocaust. How could Jews really be the cause of terrorist attacks?

I would answer such a question by pointing to history and the phenomena of historical causality. History can be defined in terms of set of actual events that are bound in the process of cause-and-effect. In this light, I would argue that the fact of the Holocaust was a cause that led to a chain of events that caused English Jews to be a contributing factor to the September 11th attacks, in effect.

How could this be, you may ask? The explanation is really not that complicated. Take the historical fact that 6 million Jews were killed in the Holocaust. Now, ask yourself. What did this do to the Jewish communities? The response is simple enough. Many Jews felt anger, shock, and horror. Some Jews (and experts have pointed to a "commonality" of response among Jews) started to think that the world is no longer safe for Jews. This thought felt more real on a personal level because of the extent of Jewish deaths.

In other words, the trauma of the Holocaust became personalized in Jewish communities and among individual Jews. More importantly from a historical standpoint, Jews felt like they had to do something. Some Jews felt that they had to contribute to recording the Holocaust, either through literature or via the agency of museums and other public monuments, so that the deaths of 6 million Jews would not have been in vain or meaningless. Other Jews focused on movements, either academically, socially, or politically, to prevent any such thing from happening to Jews ever again.

On the surface, both of the responses seem positive. Isn't it good to remember the death of those who died at cruel hands? Isn't it noble to try to prevent atrocious murders from happening again? Of course, the answer is "yes" on both counts. But the problem is that the situation is not that simple. Life and human behaviors do not happen in a vacuum. There are many players in history. And it would be simply unfair to the human race to give Jews a *carte blanche*.

The problem, of course, is that Jews feel that they are entitled to a *carte blanche*. Jews often feel that the historical fact that 6 million Jews died in the Holocaust gives Jews entitlement and rights on behalf of the killed Jews. And many Jews act accordingly.

The problem is clearly visible from the outset. The fact is that Jews who live now are not the same as the Jews who were killed by Hitler. Certainly, in the 21st century, we can go as far as to argue that Jews now cannot even claim entitlement based on familial bond. To put it bluntly, Jews today do not have the right to use 6 million Jews who were killed to claim anything. But often they do. Of course, English Jews participate in this global phenomenon.

To illustrate the offense of this behavior in the minds of non-Jews, I will provide an example from common law. In English Common Law dealing with contracts, the Woodward case (*Trustees of Dartmouth College vs. Woodward 1819*) is seen as the starting point. The details of the case is not important; the principle established by the case is. The basic idea is that the person who is wronged should be the one who is suing.

In other words, the Woodward case is clear in emphasizing that in the case that **C** has been wronged by **A**, only **C** can sue **A** for restitution. **B** cannot sue on behalf of **C**, even if **B** clearly states the intent of passing the restitution onto **C**. The reason for the Woodward principle is the fear that **B** will get fat and rich off of **C**'s pains. The Common Law intend to safeguard the system from third parties enriching themselves on other people's losses. Even today, the fundamental principle of the Woodward principle is upheld, although certain exceptions are granted in exceptional cases.

It is important to realize that the reason why the Woodward case is upheld time and time again is the fundamental ethical principle in common society (and law) that it is unjust for the third party to profit off of someone else's pain. The Woodward case reflects popular, assumed ethics. In other words, it is safe to assume that an average English person of any class fundamentally assumes that a third person must not get rich of someone else's pain. In a sense, this is a part of the fundamental societal understanding of what is right and wrong.

When Jews, including English Jews, participate in a type of violation of the Woodward principle by suing on behalf of **C**, legally they go against commonly held principles. Furthermore, the problem is confirmed because it is clear that Jews who are living and suing in the name of Holocaust victims are getting rich on their tragedy. This reality is exactly why the Woodward principle has been upheld time and time again. There is a fundamental understanding of the violation of order and justice when a third party benefits from the loss of another.

When today's Jews engage in such a type of profit taking – either in concrete terms or in "soft" terms – on the death of Jews in the Holocaust, many instinctively feel that the graves of the Holocaust victims are being desecrated and social order and justice violated. Why should Jews in England today benefit by the fact of suffering of others from over 50 years ago? Why should Jews in America benefit by mentioning the death of Jews in the Holocaust? There is a fundamental perception that it is ethically wrong for today's Jews to profit from the suffering of others in the past.

Thus, today's Jews may try to convince the world that when they sue Germany or France for the Holocaust, they are doing it on the part of the dead in the Holocaust, but the argument seems fundamentally faulty in light of the Woodward case and, more importantly, in light of popular perception.

The response is easy to see. People feel that Jews are taking advantage of the system by exploiting the Holocaust. Those who were unjustly killed in the Nazi regime are used to make some contemporary Jews fat cats. It just doesn't feel right. The result is the response of anger (at Jews) and disgust at the pollution of justice and right rule of law.

In this regard, we see that the historical fact of the Holocaust set some things in motion. Jews in England and America became trigger-happy in terms of discourse and lawsuits, soliciting a response. And the response, which Jews cannot control in most cases, adversely affect them.

When ordinary Americans or British citizens feel that Jews today in their country are exploiting the Holocaust to profit financially, socially, or politically, a type of social unrest or anger rises. And as social actions and reactions go (especially seen in Hegelian terms), a conflict will certainly rise. Discontent will give vent verbally or physically.

This illustrates well how historical fact can begin a series of causes resulting in a potential tragedy. It is important to understand the cause-and-effect principle in history. It is the historical fact of Jews-as-victims that bring a chain of cause-and-effect manifestations that result in another potential historical reality. If one can understand this working of history, one can begin to grasp the possibility of how English Jews can be a cause for September 11th attacks.

Let us look more directly at the matter at hand. How does the Holocaust bring about a series of cause-and-effect sequences, whereby English Jews can be identified as a cause for the 9/11 attacks?

The Holocaust has deeply impacted the psyche of the English Jewish community as it has American Jewish communities. And English Jews have found ways in the

English context to exert themselves in response to the Holocaust. As in the American Jewish case, the response involved an aggressive pro-Israel stance on the part of English Jews. It is true that there are not strategic legal and lobbying bodies in England that are distinctively Jewish, as in the United States. As a typical person with Jewish association can attest from the numerous letters asking for donations, there many Jewish organizations that have a political or legal bent in Washington, DC, alone. The proliferation of Jewish political associations and lobby groups can be explained by the nature of US politics. Lobby groups, such as Tobacco lobbies, had a great influence in the way the Senate voted on domestic and international legislation. Jewish lobby groups became organized and numerous and lobbied effectively for Jewish interests, domestically and internationally.

For instance, many of the Jewish groups in America emphasize pro-Israel policy and try to influence Senate voting in Israel. These Jewish lobby groups are special interest, like Tobacco lobby groups, so their concern is not the good of the American people or American health. These Jewish lobby groups have one purpose and one purpose only: to push Jewish interests and get favorable legislation.

By the rules of lobby tactics, these Jewish legal and lobby groups cajole, persuade, and browbeat politicians to vote in favor of Jewish causes and Israel. Senate voting records prove that Jewish lobby groups have been very effective in pushing their interests in the similar way that Tobacco lobby groups had been. There is enough pro-Israel legislation passed by the Senate that most of the world thinks that America is pro-Israel – that includes the free world as well as the terrorists.

English politics is quite different from American politics. Lobby groups have never played such a significant role in English politics, and it doesn't seem like that's going to change in the near future. The way to influence votes at the top is not through lobby groups but by participating in the political process.

English Jews have adapted to the political climate of England effectively and have pushed Jewish and pro-Israel interests in the English government. There are Jews in English politics in both the Labour Party and the Conservative Party. Although Jews are spread out across party lines, they have tended to vote resoundingly in support of Israel.

After the Holocaust, the United Kingdom has consistently shown a pro-Israel stance, and this is due to the aggressive support by Jews who are actively engaged in politics personally.

What makes the English political scene interesting for Americans is that it is not always easy to discern who is Jewish and who is not. Whereas in America, one's religious affiliation is almost always evident, in the English context, this is not the case.

The reason for the ambiguity in the English context can be seen in popular religiosity. Whereas 100 million Americans (33% of the population) go to a Christian church every Sunday, less than 2 million (certainly less than 10% of the population) go to church in England. Furthermore, in America, even those who do not go to a church every Sunday often participate in some kind of Christian association and profess themselves openly as Christians. In the English context, this is not the case. There is a general secularism that pervades the English society, and an English person can live a life time without having to profess his Christian faith. (Some say, however, that if push comes to shove, most secular English persons will identify themselves as Christians.)

Because there seems to be a general popular lack of interest in religion, religious affiliation of politicians are not often questioned. The end result is that most people do not know what the religious affiliations of most of the nation's leaders are. This political and religious reality seems to suit Jews working inside English political structures.

English Jews have worked effectively in the English political and social contexts, and the political program in support of Israel has been pushed in subtle and overt ways.

One could argue that everyone has his own interest, and if he's in government, he will push his interest. This may be the case, but the problem rises when a program tends to have consequences.

It's one thing to vote for fox hunting because an MP (Member of the Parliament) likes to fox hunt, it's altogether something else for a Jewish MP to vote for pro-Israel policies.

In the English context, such votes for the Jewish State can have more repercussions than in America. First of all, there really isn't a visible Muslim presence in America or in American politics. That is not naturally the case in England. There are many Muslims among the populace. Some have even argued that technically there are more Muslims in England than there are Christians. The large popular presence of Muslims means that there is a large Muslim presence in the British political process.

Whereas pro-Israel policy before 9/11 would have gone relatively unnoticed or ignored in the American contexts, policies supporting the Jewish State would have run into problems in the English context.

It is important that the Jewish-Muslim conflict is global and stems from the founding of the State of Israel. It may not be inaccurate to say that were it not for the Jewish State, Muslims would have no problem with Jews.

Historically, Muslim countries have treated Jews really well. In Iran, for instance, Jews were protected and Jewish synagogues protected officially by the government since the days of the Exile in the Old Testament. Even today, Jewish synagogues are fiercely protected in Iran by the Muslim government. The only bone of contention in the Jewish-Muslim conflict is over the State of Israel.

And the Jewish-Muslim conflict is global and prominent. What this means is that Muslims who are of African or Asian descent would participate in the Jewish-Muslim conflict based on the State of Israel and side against the Jewish State. Inner communal discourse in Muslim communities, whether in Malaysia or in English Malaysian communities, is that of resentment against the Jewish state. Although this communal resentment may be confined to the community in which it is expressed, the reality exists and is important for the

Muslim communities in perceiving the world and who they are in the world.

Thus, when the English government passes pro-Israel legislation, this captures the attention and the imagination of the Muslim communities in England. And there are a lot of Muslims in England as many of the Commonwealth countries have significant Muslim contingencies. The repercussions against pro-Israel policies reverberate throughout Muslim communities in England and are communicated to Muslims outside of Europe. Just as Christians are united globally through various associations, Muslims are united globally.

And pro-Israel policies in the British government is communicated effectively by Muslims participating in the English political process to those in their Muslim community in England as well as to Muslims around the world. Given the nature of the Jewish-Muslim conflict, the reaction will not necessarily be peaceful in discourse and conclusions.

Since there is negligent Muslim presence in America and a complete absence of Muslim presence in the US government, no directly adverse response to the pro-Israel policies can be visibly discerned. In other words, there are not Muslims within the political process in the US context who can repeatedly pass on discontent to their local communities and beyond in the Muslim context.

Thus, whereas America's pro-Israel policies do not fuel personal response on an individual level or a communal level frequently, the case is completely different in England. Every pro-Israel policy is resented in the internal discourse of the Muslim communities, whether they be Malaysian or Turkish.

So, it is easy to see how English pro-Israel policy is more detrimental in reality than American pro-Israel policies. Although American pro-Israel policies may be more numerous and there is a greater strong support fuelled by effective Jewish lobby groups, it doesn't raise the ire of Muslim communities frequently or personally. There just are not many Muslims in America and there aren't many Muslims keeping a watch on a daily basis.

In England, however, Muslims are involved in a day-to-day political discourse and involvement. There are many educated and accomplished Muslims in all levels of the British political process. Even the uneducated Muslims are kept well-informed in England by those who participate daily in the English political process. The possibility for fuelling Muslim resentment is quite unlimited and there are many channels to pass on the resentment even to the heartland of Muslim nations.

In light of the demographics in England and socio-religious reality, it is quite easy to see why English Jews can contribute more effectively to a type of 9/11 scenario. Resentment is backed up by personal accounts and personal experiences in the political process. In Hegelian terms, pro-Israel policies solicit an antithesis, and the presence of Muslims in all levels of English society make the antithesis readily available.

Why don't the Muslims attack England and not America, you may ask? If, indeed, English Jews through their pro-Israel policy involvement is fuelling Muslim discontent, then is it not logical that 9/11 should have happened in London and not in New York?

I would counter this line of question by stating: "You don't shit in your own backyard." It is a crass but an effective way to illustrate my point. English Muslims are upset at pro-Jewish, pro-Israel policies of the British government. Their resentment rises, and the communal discourse takes on a collective anger. They are in England. Many of these Muslims are respectable people in England. They have families in England.

If English Muslims had a chance to express their anger in light of the Jewish-Muslim conflict, where would they encourage the attack? A city that is seen to have the most number of Jews in the world – New York City. That way, a terrorist message is sent effectively.

Although there are pro-Israel legislations, London is not seen as a Jewish city or have that many Jews living in it in relative terms.

Perhaps more importantly, if English Muslims knew that there were fundamentalist Muslims bent on terrorist action, what would they do? English Muslims, many of whom live in London, would probably prefer to have the terrorist attack strike somewhere else.

The ideal place for Muslim terrorists would be America. First of all, there are not too many Muslims in the USA. Secondly, there are a lot of Jews in America. The whole point of Muslim terrorism is to express discontent at the Jewish-Muslim conflict and the support for the State of Israel. It would be logical to strike where there are many Jews to send the proper message. English Muslim leaders, if they were consulted at all, either directly or indirectly, probably would have expressed their desire to avert attack from England to USA.

And the facts are clear. The attacks were in New York City, where there are most numbers of Jews concentrated in the world, and Washington, DC, which contains many Jewish lobby groups that compel the US government to support Israel. The terrorist attacks of September 11th clearly was intentional and contained a message that can only be deciphered in light of the Jewish-Muslim conflict, surrounding the State of Israel.

Bin Laden's message a few days before the 2004 US Elections is clear. It is not important which president is chosen. What is important is that there is a policy change.

In other words, if there is not a visible shift from the pro-Israel policy then the terrorist attacks will continue. If pro-Israel policy is abandoned visibly and clearly in terms of policy, then Bin Laden will abandon his terrorist program.

Clearly, the Jewish-Muslim conflict is at that heart of Global Terrorism. And although messages (as well as the attacks) are directed against America, it would be a mistake to ignore the role that English Jews have played in bringing Global Terrorism to form and expression.

English Jews working within the British government, both in the Conservative Party and the Labour Party, have raised a perception of "no way out" among English Muslims (and by extension to other Muslims) on a personal and experiential level. It seems like whether the Conservative Party controls the British government or the Labour Party, the British government will always support Israel.

This kind of "no way out" perception can be seen as bringing to boiling point a pro-active Global Terrorism that gave expression on September 11th.

It is important to be empathetic to both the Jewish side and the Muslim side, who are all part of the Jewish-Muslim conflict.

Jews in England (as well as in America) are reacting to the Holocaust and try to push Jewish interests. They have identified the Jewish State of Israel as a very important part of collective Jewish interest, and Jews have tried to push their government to legislate favorably for Israel. In light of the Jewish-Muslim conflict, this places the Muslims in the defensive.

English Muslims (as we remember, there are not many Muslims in America) react to pro-Jewish policies as well as to the work of prominent Jews in politics (Muslims in the political process know who the Jews are even if the general public does not know; there is a Jewish-Muslim conflict, after all).

Although English Muslims may not start terrorism, their discontent that has been communicated to Muslims around the world for decades finally finds the Hegelian solution in Global Terrorism.

English Muslims try to avert terrorist attacks from England. Bin Laden and

Company direct their attack on New York City and Washington, DC.

In looking at historical causes, we can trace it back to the Holocaust and Holocaust-compelled actions by English Jews (and American Jews). As a twisted conclusion to the Jewish responses to the Holocaust, Americans are now left forever with the collective memory of the September 11th attacks.

It is not difficult to see how English Jews contributed directly and indirectly to the rise of the Jewish-Muslim conflict. Global Terrorism should be seen as a bubbling over of the Jewish-Muslim conflict on the global scene. In other words, 9/11 attacks should be seen as a type of "no way out" response to a rising pro-Israel policy on both sides of the political spectrum, which became more keenly felt as more and more Muslims continue to participate in English politics and experience and see first hand.

DOMESTIC AGENDA

It is not only in the pro-Israel discourse that English Jews contribute to the creation of dichotomization of society. The Jewish-Muslim conflict filters over into the English society in many different ways. So, pro-Jewish discourse on the English society level adds to the discontent of Muslims and other non-Jews regarding Judaism and other issues related with Jews. It is the radical pro-Jewish discourse on the English society level that destabilizes social stability and contributes to the destabilization of other English institutions, such as the academia and the Christian church. And this process became identified around the world as a part of the English character. English academia and the English church came to be understood as pro-Jewish. The fact of exclusive support of Jews, as perceived by non-Jews and non-Jewish religions, adds to the discontent, and it festers in an open wound. And this kind of pro-Jewishness is exported by English academia and the English church to other parts of the world.

If English institutions are characterized by an explicit pro-Jewish discourse, then should not England have been attacked? Why was America attacked on September 11, 2001? Is it not more constructive to see the role American Jews have played in creating an atmosphere conducive to 9/11? It might not be a bad idea to examine for the sake of American security the role that

American Jews might have played in the provoking of the attack.

But I have decided to focus on English Jews. And I will confine myself to that focus. I would argue that it is possible to identify a causal link between a radically pro-Jewish discourse created by English Jews and the 9/11 attacks on America. The continuance of such discourse and reality certainly places America in a vulnerable position. In other words, English Jewish efforts to create a pro-Jewish discourse are a cause for September 11th attacks and raise the possibility of potential attacks for America in the future.

How could this be? If English academia is pro-Jewish and the English church is pro-Jewish, how does this reality link to terrorist attacks against America? Before answering this question, it would be wise to examine the pro-Jewish nature of English academia and the English church. It is only from the vantage point of informed understanding that we can venture to understand the link to Global Terrorism directed at America on September 11, 2001.

How is English academia pro-Jewish? There are many factors that indicate the pro-Jewish nature of English academia. First, I will examine the academic discourse. In the English speaking world, writing about the Holocaust and anti-Semitism proliferated in the last several decades. There was the general perception created that anti-Semitism is the greatest kind of evil. Academic writing directly purporting this position (and inferring this position) came from the United Kingdom and the USA. Majority of the scholars pushing this agenda have been Jewish, either by self-defined ethnicity or by religious definition. Although it can be argued that American Jews created the biggest corpus of literature in this category, British Jews are not far behind. To a large extent, it is safe to assume that a type of normative ethics has developed that radically criminalizes anti-Semitism or anything resembling anti-Semitism in the academic context.

The key point to emphasize here is that anti-Semitism has been demonized. But the fact is, anti-Semitism is not clearly defined. To illustrate this point, is anti-Semitism killing Jews? If this is the case, not killing Jews would not be anti-Semitism. It can be cast into another category. For instance, one can argue that someone who says, "Judaism sucks!" is taking a position of anti-Judaism. But having an anti-Judaism position is not necessarily bad. People are entitled to their opinions and preferences. Also, how is saying, "Judaism sucks!" different from saying, "Hinduism sucks!"? There is no quantifiable difference between the two statements. They are both criticizing a religion. Or, to be less charged, they are both showing discontent for a religion.

In other words, it is not more evil to say, "Judaism sucks!" If we are going to put a negative value judgement, the two statements should be seen as equally negative. The anti-Semitism discourse created by Jews in English (and American) academia puts a qualitative spin on it. By using the term anti-Semitism, Jews have made it sound like it is more evil to say, "Judaism sucks!" As a Hindu, I find this personally very offensive. I resent the fact that Jews in academia use a term that is not clearly defined to make their religion seem superior to my religion.

It is important to think critically about the term. Anti-Semitism. What is it? The way Jews in England (and America) have come to define it is in functionalist ways. A person is deemed to be anti-Semitic if she says anything critical of Jews or Judaism. Thus, for example, if a Hindu woman criticized the idea that Judaism sees Jews as a chosen race, then this Hindu woman is seen as anti-Semitic. Also, if a feminist objects to Judaism's emphasis that Jewish women are ritually impure practically half the month because of having a monthly period, then this feminist woman is deemed to be an anti-Semite. Anti-Semitism has taken on a nebulous state, and it is used as a mechanism to bully and beat anyone who thinks critically about Judaism as a religion.

In other words, the epithet of anti-Semite has become a totalitarian tool to keep people quiet. No one is allowed to think critically about Judaism without suffering political repercussions in the academia. A Hindu who critically examines Judaism will be branded an anti-Semite, and she will be summarily dismissed from job opportunities and promotion in academia.

Jews in England (and in America) have used the accusation of anti-Semitism to rise in power (personally and collectively as Jews) and to maintain suppression of others, such as a critically-thinking Hindu. Jews in England (and in America) have functionally succeeded in criminalizing "anti-Semitism" and making it a political tool for the advancement of the members within the Jewish community (loosely defined).

Of course, the agenda to criminalize anti-Semitism (loosely defined) has had a deep impact on academic inquiry. It is not inconceivable that much historical data have been manipulated to push a pro-Jewish program in academia. It is a near certainty that a lecture course on World War 2 will be biased in favor of Jews with the strategic goal to push a totalitarian-type illegalizing of critical thinking on Jews and Judaism in the modern context. As such a program became normative in English history faculties and in America as well, a type of intellectual totalitarianism came to exist in the English-speaking world.

In sum, anti-Semitism bashing in in English academia (and American academia) can be found on two levels. First, in direct academic discourse, there is a type of silent totalitarian invective against any critical thinking on Jews or Judaism. Secondly, there is a popular level injunction in academic social settings. What I mean by this is that it has become unfashionable or even obscene to talk critically about Jews and Judaism in social settings in universities. There is always the social stigma of being branded as an anti-Semite, and Jews in universities are never patient about indiscriminately applying the charge or threatening to apply the charge.

The reality of the English academia is clear. There is a visible copulative intercourse principle at play between anti-Semitism and the greatest academic evil. Any critical thinking about Jews and Judaism is anti-Semitic, so the implicit argument goes. And anti-Semitism is the greatest academic evil in the classroom and outside it. This aggressively pro-Jewish reality in English academia has been consciously and proactively created by English Jews. Even today, such aggressive pushing of this principle and a rabid witch-hunt for the so-called anti-Semites are clearly visible in English universities. Thus, witnesses to this reality abound everywhere.

It is not only in English academia that there is a pro-Jewish stance that is visibly pervasive. Another English institution that has proven to be aggressively pro-Jewish is the English church. The pro-Jewish stance of the Church of England deserves some attention. Why is it that the Church of England is pro-Jewish?

On a basic level, the answer relates to power. The Church of England is a socio-political institution (besides being a religious institution) that has a long history in the history of England. During this long period, the Church of England has enjoyed an important place in the English society. And even today, the Church of England practices significant power at the highest levels of the English society, even though actual attendance of the populace in church services is less than 5% of the population.

The fact is that the Church of England is tied to the Constitutional Monarchy. Even today, the appointment of the head of the Church of England is done with a direct, active involvement of the English Parliament and the Prime Minister. Thus, the selection process of the current head of the Church of England, Rev. Rowan Williams, the Archbishop of Canterbury, was conducted with the active involvement of Prime Minister Tony Blair and the Labour Party government.

The power does not flow only from the state to the church. The state has often looked to the Church of England for ethical sanction of its activities. Although the Church of England has not always supported the English government, the English government desires its support. It is a matter of soft power. And the English government knows that it cannot provide moral sanction for itself. The Church of England is the ideal third party to give the moral nod, given its place in English history and cultural experience.

Because the Church of England became linked to the English government in direct and indirect ways, those who wanted power worked to manipulate the link. English Jews as a group have not been slow to access this channel of power. It is not difficult to find Jews in the Church of England structure. There are true converts to Christianity to be sure, but there are so-called converts who are actually advancing Jewish interests in the Church of England structure itself.

This is done in several ways. First, there are Jews who married Christian leaders. Unlike the Roman Catholic Church, the Church of England is not very strong in emphasizing the principle that Christians should marry Christians. This laxity of the fundamental historic Christian rule upheld by the Catholic Church is found at the highest levels of the English church. Thus, it is not surprising for Anglicans to find even a head of a major Cathedral who is married to a woman who is not a Christian. Certainly, his wife can be Jewish, and it is not impossible to find more than a few such cases. Jewish women who are married to Anglican clergy have been known to influence Anglican discourse through the agency of their spouse who is a leader in the Church of England.

Secondly, there are more and more individuals who call themselves "Jewish" found among the Church of England leadership structure. Some of them may be identified as being like the Judaizers of the Book of Galatians in the New Testament. Judaizers in Galatians were converts to Christianity who emphasized observing Jewish traditions, such as kosher laws. St. Paul condemns Judaizers and emphasized Christian unity.

But Judaizers are not the only ones found in the Church of England structure. There are those who call themselves Jewish who do not seem to accept the deity of Jesus Christ. (In contrast, it is understood that Judaizers accepted the deity of Christ.) These Jewish leaders who are ordained clergy in the Church of England denigrate the divine nature of Christ as outlined in the Council of

Nicea and the Council of Chalcedon. Furthermore, there is a radical emphasis on the humanity of Jesus. Over-emphasizing humanity often is done with implicit rejection of the deity of Christ. Thus, it is uncommon in some churches to hear the explicit statement, "Jesus is God" or "Our God Jesus."

Thirdly, Jews have been able to access the Church of England power through social relations. There are Jew who are part of the laity in a particular Church of England. These Jews may be genuine converts or participants in congregational life without real conversion. What is important to note is that some of these Jews who are laity in a Church of England congregation practice their influence by pressing a pro-Jewish agenda in Bible study discussions. Also, a pro-Jewish influence is exerted in social settings with weak-minded Christians who do not have a real link with Judaism. It is possible that pro-Jewish influence exertion is done on an unconscious level by Jewish individuals. But we cannot dismiss the possibility that a conscious, even strategic, pro-Jewish influence is exerted in the Church of England context.

There are several factors that have made it easier for English Jews to exert influence in the Church of England. Perhaps the greatest factor is the pro-Jewish nature of English theologians. English theologians tend to write in a very pro-Jewish way. This may be influenced by the general pro-Jewish trend in English academia. Since there is a social stigma attached to criticizing Jews and Judaism, and a type of totalitarian punitive system is in place in universities, English theologians cowtow to the pressure.

Even if some English theologians want to conduct critical thinking on Jews and Judaism, they are afraid to. There is a type of Stalinist-Leninist type environment when it concerns Jewish issues. There is so much to lose in the current university climate, so many English theologians refuse to publish anything that is overtly critical of Jews and Judaism.

But it is not merely the general academic climate that is at play. There are Jewish scholars in theology departments and ancillary departments, such as Oriental Studies or Near Eastern Studies, which exhibit a vested interest in defending Judaism and attacking Christianity. In other words, there is a hand-to-hand combat situation in academia. A Christian theologian who is critical of Jews and Judaism can often be sure to receive some form of social or political blow from Jewish professors.

Jewish professors have proven that they are capable of using the security of their position and accessible institutional power to punish academics who are critical of Jews and Judaism. Such aggressive tactics are often directed at academics who show even the remotest support of others who are willing to think critically about Jews and Judaism. It would not be wrong to describe the existence of warfare in universities on the issue of Jews and Judaism. The ones who are consciously and aggressively waging the war are Jews.

Often, Christian scholars are too unprepared or lack the courage to resist. The result is a lack of body of writing on Jews and Judaism conducted critically. Of course, to be fair, it is not easy for Christian theologians to make their stance because the general academic environment is quite totalitarian in favor of Jews at the present time. Of course, things can change in the future.

Besides the anti-Christian (and pro-Jewish) pressure in academia, there are other factors that have a bearing on uncritical thinking about Jews and Judaism among English theologians. There are Jews writing pro-actively about Jews and Judaism. Many are aggressively pushing a pro-Jewish vision even in the realm of Christian studies. The best example of this is found in the writing of Professor Geza Vermes of Oxford University.

Professor Geza Vermes has published a book entitled, *Jesus the Jew*. As the title indicates, the whole book is an effort to put Jesus inside Judaism. Bluntly put, it is a way to subjugate Jesus under the authority of Judaism. It can certainly be argued that Vermes, who converted to Judaism from Christianity, has an agenda to push. *Jesus the Jew*, therefore, can seen as a propaganda tract to convert Christians to Judaism. And since the publication of *Jesus the Jew*, Professor Vermes has published numerous articles and books pushing his agenda.

By in large, Professor Vermes has exerted great influence in English theological discourse. First of all, he has produced Ph.D.'s who are converted to his theological vision. Secondly, he has taught at Oxford University and has had a position of influence in the United Kingdom among academics working in the field. Thirdly, legions of undergraduates have bought into the agenda and are active in many areas of English life, including the government and journalism.

Thus, besides the negative pressure against critical thinking on Jews and Judaism, the force of Professor Vermes' work in the English context has set the tone for a pro-Jewish discourse in the Church of England. There is currently no English theologian who has provided alternative position on the Jewish question at the same level of discourse.

Because English theologians are functionally pro-Jewish (and loath to be critical of Jews and Judaism) due to pressure and aggressive pro-Jewish propaganda party, they participate in creating an atmosphere in the English church where Jews are free to exert Jewish influence without any resistance or opposition. It may even be stated bluntly that it is impossible to locate active and explicit critical thinking about Jews and Judaism in any English church. The end result is that Jews practice significant power through the agency of the Church of England. In other words, Jews have effectively tapped into the power of the English church, which is linked to the English government.

It is clear that English academia is pro-Jewish. It is clear that the English church is pro-Jewish. Jews have won their wars on both fronts to push an aggressive pro-Jewish agenda. The Jewish success is so thorough that now there is even a social stigma attached to criticizing Jews and Judaism even on a casual social levels in the realms of the English academia and the English church. Although things can change, this is the current climate.

How does this social reality in the United Kingdom contribute to the advancement of global terrorism? More in line with the title of the book, how did the state of affairs in England contribute to the reality of 9/11? In other words, how did English Jews (and what they have accomplished) contribute to September 11th attacks on America?

The answer on a simple level is discontent. There is a reason why people hate oppressive totalitarianism. Even if people are bullied into not expressing their thoughts or conducting critical examination, their inner discontent cannot be forced into oblivion. And the inner discontent can fester and explode. As more and more individuals experience this discontent, their discontent becomes collective. Even if there isn't an active discontent on the topic, individual discontent is shared by the virtue of the fact that their individual experiences are similar in this regard. Thus, we can speak of a collective discontent. This collective discontent can fester on individual levels and explode in a domino effect – in a spontaneous combustion at any time.

Terrorism can be seen as a result of such a discontent. It is clear that global terrorism cannot be conducted without highly educated individuals. And it has been shown that leaders in the Taliban include Oxford University and Harvard University graduates, who have distinguished themselves in their disciplines. It is not surprising that some of them experienced the collective resentment that is implicit in an oppressive, totalitarian setting where no critical thinking of Jews and Judaism is allowed (in effect).

Instead of positively channelling their discontent, for instance through artistic or literary expression or social action, these discontent individuals have opted for the negative channel of violent resistance through terrorism. Although we cannot support terrorism on the global level, it is important to understand what caused this trend. And it is important to recognize that some discontent intellectuals who had experienced oppression of the totalitarian-type have opted for the negative channel. It is not surprising that these intellectuals are Muslims who are aware of the Jewish-Muslim conflict. For, these Muslim intellectuals, either educated in the West or aware of the Western climate, resent a totalitarian-type support for Jews and Judaism in essential institutions of the West.

As terrorist cells form and become highly organized with the help of Muslim intellectuals, they look for targets. United Kingdom certainly can be a terrorist target. So, it is possible to recognize the possibility of a wide-scale terrorist attack on the United Kingdom in the near future thanks to the bursting of discontent in the Muslim world in light of aggressive pro-Jewish environment in the United Kingdom. For 9/11, however, the Muslim terrorists chose the United States.

It is certainly true that Muslims tend to be more aware of the environment in the United Kingdom than the United States. There are more Muslims in England than in the USA. To illustrate this, one only has to look at Cambridge University. There are something like 1,000 Muslim students registered with Muslim organizations. In contrast, the Christian Union enjoys less than 500 members university-wide. The ratio of 2:1 is accurate on the general English society level as well.

It is true that Muslims are more aware of the English setting, aggressively pushed in the pro-Jewish direction by the active work of key English Jewish players. Although there are not many Muslims in America, there are enough to be aware of the pro-Jewish trends of American universities. The Muslim discontent might have experienced more wide collective discontent on the English setting or a setting that is close to the English setting (like in Pakistan and Malaysia), but terrorism took on a global identity.

Perhaps, because there are many Muslims in the United Kingdom, especially in London, it seems understandable why Muslim terrorists prefer to attack areas where there are less Muslims. And the 9/11 attacks showed that they were strategically targeting areas which had greater concentration of Jews than not.

In other words, Muslim terrorism might have been fuelled more by the experiences of realities in the English context but the expression of that collective discontent was realized in the American setting, where there is a greater concentration of those who are responsible for the discontent. Thus, September 11th attacks should be seen in the context of the Jewish-Muslim conflict that has reached the height of global expression.

To put it another way, the 9/11 attacks were not necessarily attacks on America. The terrorist attacks on September 11th were attacks on Jews in light of the Jewish-Muslim conflict. But the September 11th attacks were also a form of protest against the British and American governments for a pro-Jewish position (or what Muslims perceived as a pro-Jewish position). This is confirmed in the video tape of Bin Laden before the 2004 US Presidential Elections. Bin Laden states that it is not important who gets elected; what he cared about is a policy change. Indeed, Muslim discontent is based on the perception and personal experiences of Muslims living in England (and in America), who perceive aggressive pro-Jewish agenda that seems to yield totalitarian-type power on official and social levels.

Are English Jews responsible for September 11th attacks? Yes, at least indirectly. It is true that English Jews did not hold guns to Muslim heads to start terrorism. But in light of the tensions mounting from the long-standing Jewish-

Muslim conflict, what English Jews have done to advance Jewish interests in England amounted to a declaration of war on Muslims, both in England and outside of it. Many Muslims acted on the perceived declaration of war, some positively through social activism and artistic endeavors. Unfortunately, there were others who chose the venue of aggressive, terrorist violence against America to express their popular discontent at what they perceived to be a type of totalitarian support of Jews.

So, yes, English Jews are at least partly responsible for the 9/11 attacks on America. And there is ample evidence even now that such a trend for aggressive Jewish propaganda is not abating in England. Just examine Oxford University and Cambridge University carefully, and you will have ample proof of this social/political reality.

ENGLISH JUDAISM

Certainly, not all English Jews are bad people. In fact, I like a lot of the English Jews whom I have met. But as the saying goes, "The road to hell is paved with good intentions." In the case of Jews, this is unfortunately true. And for the Americans who have suffered as the result of September 11th attacks, this is particularly felt in a real sense. English Jews could have all the good intention in the world, if what they do contributes to terrorist attacks on America (or England), there is a big problem. There may be many well-intentioned things that English Jews do that could contribute directly or indirectly to the growth of global terrorism. But I would like to focus on the area of Jewish religion in this section.

In other words, I would like to ask the question: What is it that English Jews do in the area of Jewish religion that contributed to the 9/11 attacks on America? In order to answer this question, some space has to be given to understanding English Judaism and Jews in the English context.

It would not be wrong if we said that the majority of English Jews are secular. Jews in England are not shaped by overarching religiosity or devotion to the Jewish religion. This is not to say that there are not orthodox Jews in England. There are. But the majority of English Jews are non-religious or minimally religious. This reality can be understood primarily in light of

English history and Jewish history in the English context.

Jews have been living in England for a long time. There are Jews who have been living in England since the Roman Empire, and they have been living in England continuously until the expulsion of Jews from England in 1290 AD. And soon afterwards, when Jews were allowed to return, many did. So it is technically possible to find a Jew in England who can trance their lineage all the way back almost a 1,000 years.

It is safe to assume that many Jews intermarried during that time. So, it is not surprising to meet an English Jew who looks completely Anglo-Saxon. As we know, Jews are a Semitic people. A Jew should technically look like an Arab person from the Middle East. And many Sephardic Jews still do. But English Jews cannot really be said to be racially Semitic any longer. In terms of race, it may be more appropriate to say that English Jews tend to be more Anglo-Saxon than not.

If English Jews are not racially Jews and many tended not to be religiously Jewish, then how are they Jewish? Several words have been thrown around to describe Jewishness in England. One significant category is culture. Some Jews have opted to identify themselves as culturally Jewish. What this means is that English Jews are

Jews by the virtue of the fact that they observe certain Jewish customs and traditions. So, for instance, some secular Jews may have a Hanukkah party or celebrate Rosh Ha-Shanah. It is important to note that the emphasis on Jewishness as a culture is more prominent in America than in the United Kingdom.

Another category has been thrown around to indicate the Jewishness of English Jews; namely, ethnicity. Some have posited that English Jews are Jews ethnically. This claim seems to bypass the problem of race. It is harder to argue that Jews are Jews racially in light of predominant and visible racial mixture. However, arguing for Jewish ethnicity seems simpler because ethnicity is not racially bound. In fact, ethnicity as a concept is open enough (whereas race is not) that it can be catered to describe Jewishness more fluidly.

Allow me to illustrate my point. A Jew can argue that he is Jewish ethnically because he sees his identity bound up in Jewish traditions and because he feels a bond with his Jewish heritage. Although this seems like saying a lot, it really isn't. There is no real concrete bond. The weakness of the bond is highlighted when one asks the question: Is a Christian who has no Jewish connection whatsoever "eth-nically Jewish" if he feels a bond with Jewish traditions and Jewish heritage? The answer would be no. It doesn't matter how much bond the Gentile may feel with Jewish traditions and Jewish heritage. He is not technically Jewish in terms of ethnicity. It is possible to see the confusion that could arise with this category.

But the assumption is there (and seems to be bound by a type of social contract) that only Jews will claim Jewish ethnicity. It is possible to see why some may feel that Jewish identity languaged in terms of ethnicity may sound circular.

However, it is the precise openness of the definition that allows the ethnicity category to include English Jews regardless of religious affiliation and racial composition. Although it is difficult to use the category of ethnicity for quantifiable tests (how many Jews are living in London, for instance?), it is a functional category that works on a societal level and often works even on the level of academic discourse. Certainly, on an academic level, there may be a type of delineating the bounds (or the definition) of Jewish ethnicity.

Perhaps, closely related with the idea of ethnicity is the concept of the Jewish nation. Jewish national identity (otherwise known as Zionism) is, however, quite different from the definition of Jewish ethnicity. Jewish ethnicity does not require a separate Jewish state. Even the most assimilated Jews can claim Jewish ethnicity, whereas they would most likely not want to call themselves Zionists. Zionism implies a certain nationalist outlook that often runs into conflict with Jewish citizenship in the Diaspora.

Another factor that disturbs liberal Jews is the fact that Zionism is a right-wing ideology that was given birth from the pool of right-wing European nationalism in the 1800s. Many liberal and assimilated Jews want to extricate themselves from what they perceive as a racist ideology of Zionism. Defining Jewish identity in terms of ethnicity allows them to do this.

But for all practical purposes, there isn't an identifiable movement of Jewish group identity based on Jewish ethnicity category. In contrast to Zionism, which almost seems to require a visible partici-pation in an identifiable Zionist group or movement, Jewish ethnicity category is quite passive. It can be seen as similar to a Danish person who is an English citizen. His grandfather is Danish, but for all practical intents and purposes, he is English. He may still have a Danish name, but that is not so important to his personal identity. He may, in fact, say that he is ethnically Danish, but he doesn't think about it too much. He considers himself English, first and foremost.

For most assimilated Jews, a subtle Jewish identity suits them. And the eth-nicity category does allow a more overt identification with Judaism as well, so it is possible for those Jews who want to assert their Jewishness more aggressively to do that. The only possible disadvantage with this category is that there is no real identifiable group of Jews who are defined ethnically (contra Zionism). Thus, it is diffi-cult to study Jews as an ethnic group.

What is identifiable in the English society are those who are religiously Jewish. So I will examine Jewish religious group identity in an effort to answer the question: How did English Jews contribute to the September 11th attacks in America? The focus will be on English Judaism.

There are two main categories of religious Jews in England; namely, orthodox and reformed. Next few paragraphs will be devoted to explaining these two categories. First, I will examine orthodox Jews. Orthodox Jews can be defined as those who observe the Jewish Law. Jewish Law is typically contained in the rabbinic writings of the Mishnah which is accompanied by a larger body of commentaries on the Mishnah, called the Talmud. The Talmud contains expositions of various rabbis on the points of the Mishnah. There are many dissenting opinions but the general trend in inter-pretation can be divided as tending toward Hillel, a more liberal rabbi from the ancient world, or tending toward Shammai, a more conservative rabbi. Although they disagree on particular emphasis of the Jewish Law, both of them fundamentally uphold the main principle of the Jewish Law and this is clear in the rabbinic writing. Both the Hillel camp and the Shammai camp emphasize radical observance of the law.

In a sense, therefore, it can be said that Judaism as defined by rabbinic texts is about observing the Jewish law. There are two Talmuds, the Palestinian Talmud and the Babylonian Talmud. The name is due to the location of the composition process. The Babylonian Talmud was compiled around 500 AD in Babylonia, or present-day Iran. The Palestinian Talmud was compiled and written down in Palestine a few hundred years later near the region of present-day Syria. The Mishnah was composed near the present-day Syria around 200 AD.

It should be remembered that the Roman Empire kicked Jews out of Jerusalem in 70 AD, and made it unlawful for Jews to return to Jerusalem. There is practically no evidence of Jews returning to Jerusalem during the period of the Roman Empire and centuries beyond.

Although two Talmuds exist, Jewish communities have practically abandoned the Palestinian Talmud for the Babylonian Talmud. Rabbinic Judaism through the centuries has depended on the Babylonian Talmud for religious observance and communal life. This trend persists today.

Orthodox Jewish communities in England likewise depend on the Babylonian Talmud to guide religious life. Legal observance is important for English Jews as it has been for rabbinic Jews for centuries. The importance of observing the Jewish Law is so significant that it may almost be argued that it is more important to observe the Jewish Law than it is to believe in the Jewish deity.

In other words, religious leaders in Judaism prefer that a Jew practice the Jewish law even if he does not believe. To put it in an extreme form, it is possible to be an atheist (one who does not believe in God) and practice rabbinic Judaism. There is a radical emphasis on keeping the Jewish Law and less on believing in God.

It is clear to see the difference between Judaism and Christianity. Although Christianity emphasizes living according to the Law of Christ, what makes a person Christian is the fact that he has accepted Jesus Christ as God and is baptized. Christianity is not about observing the Christian Law but about believing in the Truine God of Christianity. Thus, it is theoretically possible to break all the laws of the Law of Christ and still be Christian. Being a Christian is defined as believing that Jesus is God.

This reality is clear in the practice of the Roman Catholic Church. There is a system of confessions in place. When a Christian sins, he can confess his sins and all his sins will be forgiven by the blood of Jesus Christ, given as a substitutionary sacrifice on the cross. Thus, a sinning Christian can go to the church and confess his sins to a priest and in the process confess his sins to the Triune God of Christianity. After the prayer of confession, his sins will be forgiven by Jesus Christ, and this declaration of forgiveness will be relayed by the priest. The system of forgiveness of the repentant is an integral part of the Christian system.

Baptist churches in America are similar in the emphasis that through the cross there is forgiveness. This is most visible in the case of former US President Bill Clinton. Bill Clinton was caught in a compromising position with an American Jewish woman, named Monika Lewinski. President Bill Clinton admitted to a type of extramarital affair with her. The Christian America was appalled at the violation of the holy bond of matrimony.

What did President Bill Clinton, a Southern Baptist, do? He went to a local Christian church and prayed a prayer of confession. President Clinton publicly declared his confessions. The response of the Baptist clergy was absolution of President Clinton's sins. President Clinton confessed his sins to the Triune God of

Christianity, and his sins were forgiven. Southern Baptists recognized the forgiveness of the sin. It is fundamentally possible and normal in Christianity to recognize the forgiveness of sins. Christianity is not about legal observance, but fundamentally about believing that Jesus Christ is God and that there is complete forgiveness through the sacrificial death of Jesus Christ on the cross. It is easy to see the fundamental difference between Judaism and Christianity. Judaism is about keeping the Jewish Law and not so much about faith. Christianity is all about faith in Jesus Christ. Everything else is secondary.

The English orthodox Jewish community is fundamentally faithful to the principles of the Jewish religion as outlined in rabbinic literature. What are the key Jewish Laws? Perhaps, the most well-known Jewish Law is the law of kashrut. Jews must eat kosher foods. There is a list of unkosher foods that can be found in Jewish religious texts. An example of unkosher food is pork. Jews who observe the Jewish Law are not allowed to eat any pork products.

But kosher laws are not only about not eating certain things. Certain things can be rendered unclean by mixture. For instance, mixing meat and dairy products is unkosher. It doesn't matter if the meat is kosher. Thus, if a Jew eats a steak and has an ice cream for desert, he has violated the law of kashrut and has become unkosher. This is an important principle. It is so important that most observant Jews have two sets of utensils – one to be used with meat products and another to be used with dairy products.

Another important Jewish Law that is central to the Jewish religion is the observance of the Jewish Sabbath. Jewish Sabbath day starts from around sunset on Friday and ends around sunset on Saturday. During this time period, a Jew is not allowed to use electricity or do any kind of work. Sabbath laws are particularly treasured in the Jewish religion because not observing Sabbath laws is considered to be a legitimate justification for God to punish Jews and even annihilate them.

Orthodox Jews fundamentally belive in the right of divine retribution. Sabbath day law is a central law in rabbinic Judaism, and the violation of it more than any other law would hasten the divine retribution, which includes the possibility of annihilation of Jews by the agency of foreign armies. This point is clearly outlined in Jewish religious texts.

Orthodox Jewish communities in England, like orthodox Jewish communities elsewhere and throughout history, have emphasized the observance of the Jewish Law. In order to observe the Jewish Law effectively, orthodox Jews consciously and systematically form orthodox neighborhoods. This way, each orthodox Jew can pressure other orthodox Jews from violating the Jewish Law. Especially since breaking of the Sabbath and other central laws are seen as legitimate justification for God to carry out annihilation-type retribution against Jews, such a system of check is seen as essential to Jewish survival.

Besides the necessity of the check-system, there are practical considerations. Jewish Laws, such as kosher laws, require ritual slaughter of animals for the meat to be kosher. Systematically forming Jewish neighborhood allows for the kosher meat butcher to set up a business that is viable. There is ready access to kosher food for orthodox Jews.

Also, because there are strict regulations for the Sabbath, including the distance one is allowed to travel, having a Jewish neighborhood allows Jews to have ready access in keeping with Jewish Laws. Thus, Jews would not break the Sabbath law by travelling long distances on a Sabbath. There are friends and family nearby, so Sabbath day can be observed in a communal way that provides ready social interaction and entertainment within the bounds of the Jewish Law.

It is not difficult to identify orthodox Jewish neighborhoods in England.

Surprisingly, the biggest orthodox Jewish neighborhood is not in London, although there are pockets of orthodox Jewish neighborhoods in London. The biggest orthodox Jewish community is in Newcastle in northern England. It is important to recognize that orthodox Jews in England (and elsewhere) emphasize keeping the Jewish Law and systematically form Jewish neighborhoods that are orthodox in nature.

Orthodox Judaism is not the only expression of Judaism in England. Another identifiable group in English Judaism is reformed Judaism. There is an identifiable number of reformed Jews in England, although not as many as in the United States, in terms of number or percentage. In America, it is estimated that there are 1 million reformed Jews or roughly about 1/6 of the American Jewish population. The situation in England is different.

First of all, not too many Jews in England are religious at all. Whereas it is important to be religious in America – to belong to some religious association – such a social expectation is not there in England. In America many secular Jews have a membership in a reformed synagogue even if they may not participate in any significant way because it is expected that everyone has some sort of a religious affiliation. Not having a religious affiliation is frowned upon in America.

A part of the reason can be found in the fact that the founding of America is seen to have been done for a religious reason – to freely practice religion. Another cause for the emphasis in being religious can be seen in the reality of the Cold War. The Communists of Russia were atheists, and America was anti-Communist in the Cold War. Americans defined themselves against Communism and in the process defined themselves against atheism.

England did participate in the Cold War, but was not as anti-Communist as America was as a government or as a people. America had the McCarthy era; England did not.

But, most significantly, evangelicalism did not sweep across England as it did in America. Currently, President George W. Bush can be seen as a Fundamentalist Christian president. But he is not alone.

Both President Ronald Reagan and President Jimmy Carter were evangelical Christians, if not Fundamentalist. And President Ronald Reagan actively courted the Christian Right, and now the Christian Right is staunchly grabbing hold of the American government. The social result of the past few decades is obvious. And for the Christian right, it is better to be a theist than an atheist.

The difference between America and the United Kingdom explains, in part, the reason for the greater presence of reformed Jews in America.

Although there are not many reformed Jews in England, they are an identifiable group with a visible presence. Particularly, it is possible to find reformed Jews in secular university settings. What is reformed Judaism?

Reformed Judaism is a fairly recent phenomena and its origins can be traced to Germany a couple of hundred years ago. Reformed Judaism started out as a way to capture the modern Jew and prevent him from leaving Judaism. The strategy of reformed Judaism can be identified as (1) providing a rationale for the Jewish religion in the modern context, (2) developing Jewish religiosity along modern lines, and (3) making Judaism respectable to non-Jews. I will examine these points in greater detail.

First of all, reformed Judaism that started in Germany tried to provide a rationale for the Jewish religion in the modern context. The purpose was to prevent educated Jews from leaving Judaism. And this fear was justified. The German society quickly became secularized after the Protestant Reformation under Martin Luther's leadership. There was an emphasis that an individual has the fundamental right to choose his own religion. This emphasis can be seen as strategic. Basically, every Christian was Roman Catholic so the

Lutherans wanted to encourage people to choose the Lutheran denomination. The argument for choice followed its logical conclusion, and the German society became highly secularized. Even having a religion at all became the choice of an individual.

In this secular climate, many opted to be non-religious. There were some Jews opting in this direction as well. German Jewish religious leaders became worried. But some Jewish religious leaders also became secularized. A combination of historical forces coupled with a genuine concern for Jewish religious expression resulted in the founding of the reformed movement. Jewish religious leaders who identified with the reformed Jewish movement tried to justify the need for a Jewish religiosity in the modern context. Such writings can be seen as a type of justification to convince educated Jews to be a part of the Jewish religious expression.

In the process of justifying the Jewish religion, reformed Judaism made conscious changes to traditional Judaism. And this leads to the second point. Reformed Jewish religious leaders strategically developed Jewish religiosity along modern lines.

For instance, reformed Jews abandoned the strict observance of the Jewish Law. In fact, some reformed Jewish leaders discouraged the observance of kosher laws and Sabbath laws. Instead, the Jewish religion was developed along philosophical lines. There were many highly educated and intelligent Jews who were capable of thinking along theoretical lines. Some of them actively participated in the development of the Jewish religion using modern philosophy and in light of the emphasis on human reason. Thus, reformed Judaism allowed individual Jewish religiosity along the lines that are found in Christianity. Reformed Judaism was concerned less about the observance of the Jewish Law and more about the understanding of the self with Judaism as a (tangential) reference point.

In reformed Judaism, even religious rituals showed abandoning of traditional rabbinic Judaism. Hebrew use was abandoned, and all Jewish services were conducted in German. And there was active changes in the religious liturgy. In other words, traditional Jewish liturgy was not just translated from Hebrew to German. Essentially, new liturgy was written in German with traditional Judaism in the background. Some reformed Jewish synagogues introduced hymns. These hymns were sung in reformed Jewish synagogues in the same way (with musical instruments) that Christians sang hymns at the Lutheran church down the street. Orthodox Jews in Germany decried what they called the desecration of Judaism. Orthodox Jews and reformed Jews grew further and further apart in Germany.

Many historians, however, regard the reformed Judaism movement in Germany as a success story. It is not difficult to see when we examine the numbers. It is true that if reformed Judaism did not exist, many Jews would have completely assimilated into the secular German culture. In places where reformed Judaism was slow to take hold, secular Jews have completely assimilated. This is evident in Scandinavia and parts of France. Certainly, reformed Judaism was the reason why hundreds of thousands, if not millions, of Jews remained within the bounds of Judaism around the world.

But perhaps more significant is the argument that reformed Judaism made Judaism respectable in the Enlightenment era. The importance of this advancement is difficult to quantify, but its significance is more crucial than many give it credit for. And this leads into the third point. Reformed Judaism made Judaism respectable to non-Jews. In effect, reformed Judaism served to provide positive advertisement for Jews.

It is not surprising why Enlightenment period Europeans would have had a problem with Judaism of the traditional kind. The idea that there were foods that could not be consumed because of a divine decree seemed to fly at the face of reason. It was irrational to argue that a perfectly edible food should not be consumed even if people may die of hunger as a result. Such ideas in Judaism seemed to insult humanism and the emphasis on human survival.

Furthermore, the fact that kosher laws insulted German customs of consuming pork did not work positively in the German society. Especially, as the German society became more and more secular and Gentiles came in contact with Jews, Jewish Laws, such as kosher laws, became a sticking point.

Reformed Judaism discarded kosher food laws completely. And reformed Judaism tried to shift emphasis away from Humanism-unfriendly laws to Humanism-friendly ideas. If they could not locate them in traditional Judaism, they created them for modern Germany. The same was the case with Sabbath laws. Reformed Jews tried to spiritualize the idea of the Sabbath and philosophized along the lines of the goodness of God or the goodness of "rest." In essence, reformed Jews did much to make Judaism respectable to the Gentiles of their time in Germany as Philo of Alexandria did to the Egyptians and Romans of his time.

Although reformed Judaism has undergone changes since its inception in Germany several hundred years ago, fundamental tenets of reformed Judaism still holds true all over the world. Judaism should be time relevant and should change with the times to accommodate historical changes. This evolutionary outlook may not always be explicitly verbalized but is always assumed implicitly. Policy changes among reformed Jewish groups clearly indicate this fundamental philosophy of reformed Judaism.

This is the case with reformed Jews of England. In character, reformed Judaism of England can be seen as more conservative (vis-à-vis traditional Judaism) than American reformed Judaism. American Jews embraced reformed Judaism early and took it to its logical conclusions. In some areas in the USA, it would be difficult to have a kosher meal in reformed synagogue social events. Pork and shrimp abound. There have been trends recently among some reformed Jewish synagogues in America to use some Hebrew in their services, but the majority still refuse to.

In contrast, English Jews were slow to embrace reformed Judaism of Germany. This is partly due to the fact that there was already radical polarization between orthodox Jews and secular Jews in England at a time when reformed Judaism developed in Germany. Neither secular Jews nor orthodox Jews in England wanted to bring reformed Judaism in from Germany. Orthodox Jews thought that reformed Judaism would destroy all Jews. Secular

Jews disagreed with the idea that one should be religious at all.

By the time reformed Judaism picked up in England, there were other forces that kept liberalizing forces in German reform Judaism in check. One significant element is Zionism. Although Zionism as envisioned by secular Jews were non-religious, there were religious Jews who quickly added religious dimensions to it. As Zionism became more and more charged with elements of traditional Jewish religion, it provided a third-party protection against radical liberalization of the Jewish religion in the synagogue setting. Furthermore, the fact that secular Jews continued to stay away from anything religiously Jewish made the composition of the reformed Jewish movement in England more favorably inclined toward traditional Jewish religion.

Thus, although reformed Jews of England often can be found eating unkosher and breaking the Sabbath, a type of anti-Jewish Law discourse did not take hold of reformed Judaism in England as it did in Germany. In Germany and in America, reformed Jews often ridiculed orthodox Jews openly and publicly showed contempt for them. Such a reality is less common in the English context.

It must be emphasized, however, that despite the fact that reformed Judaism tended to be more conservative in England than it has been in America (or was in Germany), it still is quite oppositional to orthodox Judaism. Although reformed Judaism in England does not enjoy a very visible presence in England as orthodox Judaism does, its presence is very real and those in the know are highly aware of their visibility.

Having examined English Judaism and its identifiable expression in orthodox Judaism and reformed Judaism, we find ourselves in the position of asking the question in the beginning paragraphs. What is it that English Jews have done in the area of Jewish religion that contributed to the September 11th attacks on America?

The answer to this on a simple level is that English Judaism is anti-Christian. This is the case for orthodox Judaism as well as for reformed Judaism.

It is not difficult to see why orthodox Judaism in England is anti-Christian. After all, orthodox Judaism in England (as it is in the USA) is a direct descendant of rabbinic Judaism that has long proven to be anti-Christian. In fact, it would not be wrong to say that many rabbinic Jews throughout the whole history of Christianity frequently attacked Christianity verbally and in print. In fact, it would be accurate to say that rabbinic Judaism defined itself by being anti-Christian. In other words, the anti-Christian element in rabbinic Judaism is integral to the very identity of rabbinic Judaism itself.

This is not surprising given the origin of rabbinic Judaism. From the very beginning, rabbinic Judaism prided itself in the Jewish murder of Jesus Christ. There are clear rabbinic passages that take complete responsibility for killing Jesus Christ. Later rabbinic leaders throughout the Middle Ages even tried to argue that Jews were doing Christians a favor by killing Jesus Christ and that Christians should thank Jews for having killed Jesus Christ.

From the very beginning of rabbinic Judaism, Christianity and the Christian messiah were reviled and attacked. The New Testament is agreed with rabbinic writings on this point. The Gospel of John clearly describe Jewish synagogues kicking converts to Christianity out of Jewish synagogues. Jews did not consider Jewish converts to Christianity as being Jewish any longer, and even Jewish legislation shows this. In the Eighteen Benedictions, there is a clear command to kick Christians out of Jewish synagogues. Some date this injunction as far back as to the time of Jesus Christ. From the very beginning, rabbinic Judaism perceived itself as being in conflict with Christianity, and it was an important part of its self-definition and self-understanding.

Thus, it is not surprising that orthodox Jews in England exhibit anti-Christian attitudes, both in writings and in their common discourse.

It is understandable that the Christian claim that Jesus Christ is the Messiah promised in the Old Testament is offensive to orthodox Jews. Orthodox Jews are still waiting for the messiah to come. It is understandable why orthodox Jews would consider Christianity a big lie and Christian leaders liars.

And it is understandable why orthodox Jews resent the concept of New Jerusalem and True Israel. Christians have claimed historically that Jesus will come back again in The Second Coming and establish a New Jerusalem. New Jerusalem will be on present day Jerusalem, but it will be fundamentally different. It will be a Christian Jerusalem with Jesus Christ as the ruler. All the members will be Christians. Implicitly, it is understood that those Jews who do not submit to the authority of Jesus will be kicked out of New Jerusalem.

The concept of True Israel is even more offensive to orthodox Jews. The idea of True Israel can be traced back to Jesus Christ himself. The idea was developed further by Church Fathers from the first century AD to the third century AD. The idea of True Israel was fundamentally assumed to be true in the long history of Christianity.

The basic idea of True Israel is simple. True Israel is made up 100% of Christians. The idea is that True Israel, made up 100% of Christians, represents the people of God. Jews no longer are God's people. Jews have been rejected by God when Jews crucified Jesus Christ on the cross. Jesus' crucifixion represented the ultimate and final rejection of Jews of the true God of the Bible. And the crucifixion of Jesus represented God's rejection of the Jews as a people. In other words, God will no longer save Jews as a people because Jews are no longer God's people.

Christian thinkers often cite the Biblical passage claiming that there is no longer Jew or Gentile in Christ as a textual proof. All human beings have an equal chance of salvation as individuals. Those individuals, whether Jewish or Gentile, can be saved in the substitutionary sacrifice of Jesus Christ if they believe that Jesus Christ is God and that only Jesus can save them.

The principle of True Israel has been affirmed over and over again by Christian communities throughout the 2,000 years of Christian history. This explains why the Southern Baptists of America have vowed a few years back to convert every American Jews to Christianity. American Baptists want Jews to abandon Judaism and become

Christians, thereby becoming a part of True
Israel.

The Roman Catholic Church fundamentally operates from this historic
Christian emphasis of True Israel. In
Vatican II (1962-1965), the Vatican
affirmed the idea that Jews have been
rejected by God as a people and that
Christians are True Israel, who are
beneficiaries of the blessings promised in
the Old Testament as well as in the New
Testament.

It is easy to see why these ideas – of
New Jerusalem and True Israel – are deeply
offensive to orthodox Jews. In fact,
orthodox Jews would consider the Southern
Baptists and Roman Catholics as "anti-
Semites" for their essential ideas (without
which they can't really claim to be Christian
churches). Just as rabbinic Judaism defined
itself against Christianity, historic
Christianity has defined itself against
Judaism.

Orthodox Jews in England still
believe that Jews are the chosen people of
God. They still believe that divine promises
in the Old Testament still apply to them. So,
it is natural for orthodox Judaism and its
leaders to be anti-Christian. It is only natural, given the nature of orthodox Judaism
in England and its connection with historic
rabbinic Judaism. In fact, it would not be
wrong to say that central pillars of

Christianity are all very offensive to orthodox Jews in England. They can each be a reason for why orthodox Judaism in England is anti-Christian.

Reformed Judaism is anti-Christian as well. A part of the reason why reformed Judaism is anti-Christian is similar to why orthodox Judaism is anti-Christian. Reformed Jews resent the anti-Judaism stance of Christianity and the exclusive claim that Jesus Christ is God and the only Savior. But there is more to reformed Jewish hatred of Christianity than the religious.

As reformed Judaism took on more philosophical and historical dimensions to its discourse, it adopted some aggressively secular notions against Christianity. The Enlightenment gave the world a type of critique of Christianity and the Christian church. What reformed Jews did was to add a Jewish flavour to that critique. What I mean by this is that instead of seeing Judaism and Christianity as a bilateral conflict, reformed Jews tried to demonize Christianity with universalist principles.

In other words, Judaism set out a type of third-party principle. By introducing a third party, reformed Jews thought that they could adequately weaken Christianity and the Christian church. Thus, reformed Jews appealed to secular ethics to argue that the Christian church was unethical. A good example of this type of discourse is found in the attempted portrayal of the Christian church as having persecuted the Jews.

In other words, reformed Jews tried to portray the Christian church as fundamentally unethical by arguing that the Christian church has persecuted the Jews throughout its existence. Reformed Jews, in essence, tried to portray the Christian church as fundamentally evil. By using the principles of secular ethics, for instance, reformed Jews even demonized missionary activities of the Christian church that did not engage in forcing conversions. The argument runs that the very offer of Christian conversion is offensive to Jews. In more recent times, some reformed Jews have argued that proselytism activities by the Christian church are akin to genocide on the level of ethics.

The question for the purpose of this study is not whether such an accusation by reformed Jews is ridiculous or not. We are trying to understand why and how reformed Jews are anti-Christian. It suffices this study to see that reformed Jews have introduced a third-party principle to attack Christianity and the integrity of the Christian church.

And reformed Jews have run away with this discourse. Reformed Jews argue that Christianity is characterized by anti-Jewish sentiment and action so much so that anti-Jewish attitude can be seen as an innate part of all Christians at the deepest, even subconscious, levels. Using this argument, reformed Jews have blamed Christianity for every bad thing that has happened to Jews.

It is not uncommon to see Jews blaming Christianity for the Holocaust. Such a discourse must be seen as unsubstantiated and fundamentally rising out of an anti-Christian prejudice. The Nazi state was not a Christian state, and Hitler was not Christian. In fact, Nazis killed several key Christian leaders, whom the Christian church regard as "martyrs."

In other words, the Christian church believes Hitler to be anti-Christian, not because of what he did to the Jews but because what he did to Christians. But all this is ignored in most reformed Jewish circles. And this can be attributed to the larger framework of anti-Christian attitudes of reformed Judaism. Reformed Judaism in England is certainly a party to the encouraging of the third-party principle.

There can be a lot written about how the Christian church should respond to the third-party rule. But for the purpose of this study, it is more constructive to examine how the third-party principle grounded in the anti-Christian position is a part of the contributing causal factor for the September 11th attacks on America.

In other words, how is the anti-Christian position of English Judaism (whether orthodox or reformed) related to the 9/11 attacks on America?

I would answer that by stating that it had an indirect but very real impact. Although English Judaism is aggressively anti-Christian, the Christian response has been silence. There has been no real counter-attack. In fact, the response of the Christians have been to embrace Jews. In the eyes of third parties, it appears that despite all the anti-Christian attacks by English Judaism, English Christianity embraced English Judaism. Muslims, too, have not failed to notice this process. And this caused deep discontentment among global Muslims to grow.

It is important to remember that there is a raging Jewish-Muslim conflict. It is safe to say that the Jewish-Muslim conflict is now global and is attached to global terrorism. And it would not be wrong to say, "A friend of your enemy is your enemy."

If English Christianity becomes a friend of English Judaism, it necessarily becomes the enemy of Islam in light of the global Jewish-Muslim conflict. It is irrelevant if Muslims do not have problems with English Christians *per se*. The fact is that English Christianity has made itself the enemy of Muslims by making a type of alliance with English Jews.

It is important to be sensitive to the Jewish-Muslim conflict that has produced global terrorism. Whereas English Christians do not have to be a target in the Jewish-Muslim conflict, they have become targets through their alliance with English Jews.

In other words, English Christians can become targets of Muslim anger against Jews without knowing it – just by befriending English Judaism. It has to be emphasized again that there is a global Jewish-Muslim conflict. Every Muslim, even in the most uneducated parts of Pakistan and Malaysia, are aware of the Jewish-Muslim conflict. English Christianity should be a little bit more sensitive to this global reality that is very real to over 1 billion Muslims around the world – spread out over every continent in the world. Certainly, these Muslims do not feel that English Christians are being sensitive or fair. The discontent grows.

To add insult to injury, English Christianity is supportive of English Judaism when English Jews fundamentally attack Christianity and the integrity of the Christian church. It is bad enough to see a third party support your enemy, but when the third party does this after receiving fundamental attacks (against the third party), it is not inconceivable to see why Muslims become inflamed with rage.

Besides discontent, Muslims come to feel that they have no course of peaceful action because the third party, which should be opposed to Judaism is, in fact, aggressively supportive of it. Because English Christianity is aggressively supportive of English Judaism, Muslims can naturally think that there will be no fair arbitration in the Jewish-Muslim conflict.

Even if English Christianity has made itself an ally of English Judaism without being aware, from the perspective of over 1 billion Muslims, what is important is that English Christians have allied themselves, in effect, with Jews and made themselves into enemies of 1 billion Muslims in the context of the global Jewish-Muslim conflict.

It is understandable to see that discontent mixed with a feeling of helplessness can result in a very aggressive response. In a sense, one could argue that global terrorism can be seen as a Hegelian conclusion. Global terrorism, at least against England (and America), could have been avoided had English Christians not made themselves into allies of English Jews.

There is a global Jewish-Muslim conflict, whether we like it or not, and at the present time, it is the greatest conflict for both sides. Given that there are 1 billion plus Muslims and many Muslim states, many of which are vital for world's oil supply, this reality can be a big problem.

Certainly, from the vantage point of global terrorism and world peace, this is a problem.

Thus, indirectly highly public and visible anti-Christian stance of English Judaism has caused global terrorism to be directed at the West. Of course, a similar type situation exists in America. Many American Christians have accidentally made America the target of the Jewish-Muslim conflict by angering over 1 billion Muslims by siding with Jews.

But as noted before, there are not many Muslims in America. There are in England. What happens in England is more "real" to Muslims because English Muslims experience the reality as found in England. And the word spreads like wildfire among Muslim networks. People talk. This is true of the Christian global network and the Jewish global network. The Muslim global network is no different.

The English situation is critical because it provides direct, real, and many experiences on a personal and group levels that fuel the discontent and frustration of Muslims who are, by the virtue of the fact that they are Muslims, a part of the global conflict between Jews and Muslims. This conflict will not go away, just like the New Testament will always be important to Christians.

Yes, London could have been the target of terrorist attacks on September 11th, fuelled by discontent based on Christian-Jewish relations, exacerbated by the explicit anti-Christian stance of English Jews finding unconditional support by English Christians. But Muslim Fundamentalists (growing everyday in number) decided to attack New York and Washington, DC.

As mentioned before, a part of the reason is that New York and Washington, DC, are places with many Jews. In a way the 9/11 attacks can be seen as consistent with the Jewish-Muslim conflict.

In terms of English Jewish religious contribution, American Judaism and the American Christian response are seen to be similar to what happens in the English context. It is easy to see how America can (even by analogy) become a target for terrorism rising from the Jewish-Muslim conflict.

If America, like England, chooses to be allies of Jews even when Jews attack the fundamentals of Christianity and the integrity of the Christian church, there can be no reasoning with America (like England). They will always side with Jews. And that is unacceptable in light of the Jewish-Muslim conflict. As this perception grows in the Muslim world where more and more "normal" Muslims are going over to extreme forms of Islam, America and the United Kingdom should become more concerned and much more sensitive.

September 11th attacks showed what can happen as a result. And more can happen in the future. It should be assumed that terrorists have nuclear, biological, and chemical weapons. They can easily obtain these through links with former KGB connections. It is just a matter of time, if they have not yet found an auspicious channel to deliver and set up the needed mechanism. And it is important to remember that Pakistan, a very Muslim country, already has nuclear weapons. It is not inconceivable for Pakistan to "lose" one or two of them to the terrorists.

It is important to remember the pervading discontent in the Muslim world, augmented by a sense of helplessness resulting from the American and English response to overly anti-Christian position of English (and American) Judaism. This reality can certainly provide an inspired impetus to direct terrorist attacks on America. And that's exactly what happened on September 11, 2001. America was attacked successfully by a bunch of terrorists.

Not considering the current situation in regards to the Jewish religion in light of the Jewish-Muslim conflict can potentially result in further degeneration of the global condition. As a result, millions of Americans can die in the near future due to global terrorism inspired by the Jewish-Muslim conflict.

It is important to remember the words that came out of the horse's mouth. Bin Laden, before the 2004 US Elections, said that it is not important who becomes the US President. He will not stop unless there is a policy change. In other words (and this is extremely important for America and American security), Bin Laden will stop terrorism against America if the US President changes the policy.

CONCLUSION

September 11, 2001, will be remembered for a long time. Not since Pearl Harbor were Americans awakened in such a traumatic fashion. Just as Pearl Harbor consumed national consciousness and political discourse for a long time (and it still does), 9/11 will haunt us for many years to come.

9/11 is far worse. It was a planned terrorist attack that used the date that resembles the telephone number that Americans all over the United States dial at times of emergency. It was a deliberate way to send the message that Americans are not safe any longer.

To make the matters worse, the terrorists used American planes against Americans – commercial planes, no less. It appeared that there was nothing sacred any more. Americans were made to feel that there is no safety, no place of refuge.

9/11 will haunt Americans for a long-time. And perhaps, the collective memory of the September 11th attacks will never be expunged from the national consciousness as long as a country called The United States of America continues to exist.

However, unlike Pearl Harbor, which can be relegated to the past, 9/11 is in the ever-present. Every day, Americans wake up to fear that there might be another terrorist attack on American soil.

Every day, Americans wake up not knowing if they, their children, their parents, their relatives, their friends, and their neighbors will die by a terrorist attack.

The Global War on Terrorism is far from over. Muslim fundamentalism seems to be growing. Jewish-Muslim conflict seems to be degenerating. Yassir Arafat, a man who took the steps toward the comprehensive peace in the Middle East, is on the verge of death. Bin Laden seems undeterred from conducting his terrorist attacks.

Despite all the pessimism, however, it is important to remember that millions of more Americans have not died yet. Things can turn around and peace can be established.

In order to take positive steps in the direction of security and peace, it is important to examine possible causes and trends. It is important to understand why September 11, 2001, happened. It is important to identify elements that could lead to further threat for Americans and the good people of the world.

It is in this positive light that I have conducted this study of the possible contribution of English Jews to 9/11. Hopefully, this study will spur constructive discussion. I hope that discussion will focus on the points with the view to making the world a better place.

Let us not forget that we are in a precarious situation. There is a War on Terrorism on a global level. We have to work together to find answers and a way to safety. I hope that this book will provide the impetus in the positive direction.

About the Author

Devdas Pradesh was traumatized by 9/11 and began to research and to think about the whole event in light of history and socio-political factors in order to understand. He shares some of the fruits of his work in this book.

www.ingramcontent.com/pod-product-compliance
Lightning Source LLC
Chambersburg PA
CBHW022154080426
42734CB00006B/429